OVER CORNWALL

INTRODUCTION

Cornwall 'land of legend', that's what they say, and combined with those wonderful colour posters at the train stations, who could resist a weekend trip westward to explore its magic. Eventually my weekends became more frequent and finally joined up in the middle, (Barclays Bank SW1, to tin mining at the 340 fathom level at South Crofty)

The moors west of Exeter take you back in time, giving a hint of entering a special place where the contrast of swirling mists or blazing sun, the tiny harbours, golden beaches and tin mines clinging to the cliff edges leave you in no doubt this is different. To see Cornwall from the air only adds to its rugged beauty. Looking down from above it assumes a model like quality with a variety of colour and coastal shapes that are a photographer's delight.

Bounded by the mighty Atlantic Ocean and English Channel, Cornwall acts as giant breakwater, where the surrounding sea varies from a crystal clear state with sand and rocks shining through the water, to a raging white frenzy that atomises when it pounds the granite cliffs. Enjoy the views, live the legend!

PHOTOGRAPHERS NOTE.

My first view over Cornwall was flying a glider around the Lizard Peninsula, where from only a 1,000 ft the view was fantastic, covering from Lands End in the west to the Dodman in the east, with ships passing the Lizard Point looking like models on a boating lake. A few years later when flying a VW powered ultra light aircraft I used to carry a tiny Rollie 35 camera to record events.

Aerial photography is all about the weather. In the days of black and white, a yellow or orange filter could be used to reduce the effect of haze, but when colour became the norm the weather dictated the quality of the final result, (although the advent of the digital age improved matters). Not a problem if it is only a hobby, but when clients require pictures to order, it is another matter. In one very dry summer, green fields became yellow/brown with ancient earthworks and springs suddenly becoming visible.

For a serious aerial photographer there are no weekends or bank holidays, only good working days or waiting for the weather. In Cornwall you also have to add on the tide situation. Mainly new images have been used for this book, the colours of which will vary with the time of the day and the season, also included are some earlier shots taken on film.

Finally, we are pleased to say that this publication has been produced and printed entirely in Cornwall, and trust it conveys the splendour of this rugged land of legend.   Peter Channon

The harbour that comprises the towns of East and West LOOE was one of the big game fishing centres of Cornwall, and still has an active fishing fleet, with earlier times seeing sailing ships engaged in the transport of copper and tin ore. The town has the attraction of a rugged coastline complete with beautiful inland scenery. At the harbour mouth the famous Banjo pier overlooks the popular bathing beach, and just offshore St Georges Island is under the protection of the Cornwall Wildlife Trust, with visits available during the summer. Nestling in a twisting green valley, POLPERRO with its harbour has a magic that to many visitors typifies Cornwall. Fishing boats still operate as in earlier times, but its legendary smugglers and their clandestine activities are not in evidence these days. Although very much on the visitor trail, Polperro has managed to retain its reserved charm, and is a fine example of a beautiful Cornish harbour.

The FOWEY River winds down a steep sided wooded valley and joins the sea to make a natural haven for shipping. Fowey was a major port involved with the nearby mines, and is still active in the export of china clay. In earlier times pirates used it as a base to raid the French coast, but today a large number of pleasure boats are more in evidence. Fowey is a fine example of an early Cornish port that has not been spoilt by over development, with many original buildings, and a period waterfront.

The EDEN PROJECT blossomed out of a disused china clay pit, as a result of a vision to create a unique series of temperature and humidity controlled bio domes that have become a world famous attraction. The ability to create a diverse range of climates in one location has made this a world class centre for research and visitor education, and also the location for a Bond film.

6

CHARLESTOWN was a major china clay port of the area and its facilities were developed to serve this industry as it grew. Sailing ships could be loaded from giant hoppers, and in its heyday it would have been a hive of activity, whilst over the years several films have used the period settings. The harbour has changed very little over time, and is now home to several large sailing ships with the facilities to maintain them. The fact that it is still very much a working harbour makes a visit very interesting, with a selection of eating places and a good museum.

PENTEWAN was one of the early clay ports on this coast. Ships were able to be locked into the harbour and could be loaded whilst afloat. The harbour complex was served by its own narrow gauge steam railway that brought the clay direct from the St Austell area. Although the entrance is now blocked by sand, this charming setting sits in a time warp with many remaining features of its busy past.

MEVAGISSEY is still a fishing port, with a famous past for its involvement with the Cornish pilchard trade. The inner harbour dates back to the 15th century, with the outer piers added later to give more mooring space and protection. Tourists have now replaced the pilchards, but the character and old world charm is still there.

GORRAN HAVEN is a small 13th century fishing cove safely tucked away to the east of the Dodman Point, complete with some of its original fishing cottages. Flanked by cliffs on both sides, its sheltered position and two beaches make it a safe place to enjoy the water, but on a sunny day you need to be early to get a space.

ST MAWES sits on the beautiful Roseland Peninsula, and receives a large number of visitors by sea via the regular ferry trips from Falmouth. The small harbour is a wonderful place to drop anchor, with the clear water making for good bathing. The castle which dates back to Henry V111, was a royalist stronghold during the civil war, it is well preserved and now in the care of English Heritage. The harbour area is largely unspoilt and a real suntrap, where the rest of the world seems a long way away.

The CITY OF TRURO was one of the original stannery towns of Cornwall, and an important harbour before ships became too large. Although still navigable, the main traffic is now pleasure craft that carefully wind up the river channel.
The Cathedral, although encroached upon by modern developments, stands proud overlooking the city, with the cobbles of Boscawen Street remaining to remind us of earlier days with horse drawn wagons, and ships unloading at Lemon Quay. Very much the administration and business heart of Cornwall, Truro has had to adapt to modern times, but still has good examples of its earlier architecture.

The RIVER FAL & CARRICK ROADS are bordered on both sides by fields and woodlands, with the Truro and Fal rivers having merged upstream to eventually join the sea at this natural shipping haven. The depth of water has made it an ideal place for ships to lay up, and the King Harry Ferry serves as the gateway to the Roseland area. A truly unspoilt part of Cornwall, the contrast of colour and its inlets are unbeatable. Tolverne Cottage and Turnaware Point were both D-day embarkation points in 1944, and a Roman camp is in evidence at Roundwood Quay.

FALMOUTH is noted for its magnificent natural harbour, fine beaches and tropical vegetation. Its importance as a shipping haven prompted the building of Pendennis and St Mawes Castles during the reign of Henry V111. The famous Royal Mail packet ships sailed from here until 1852, and today fishing boats, pleasure craft, and ocean going ships combine to make it a hive of activity. A major docks complex has grown up over the years, which are capable of dry docking quite large vessels. Alongside the docks a new marina, and the National Maritime Museum have been added to the areas features, and to the south of the town a fine selection of beaches stretch around towards the Helford Estuary.

HELFORD RIVER is another example of a large wooded inlet that offers natural protection to the many boats moored there. A ferry runs across from the village to Helford Passage, with the small hamlets of Durgan and Mawnan nearby. The magnificent Trebah Gardens run down to the waters edge, and this was one of the local D-Day embarkation points for the American army in 1944. The multitude of pleasure and small fishing craft has now replaced the smuggling and sailing schooners of the past, but the classic beautiful setting is timeless.

COVERACK'S remote position at the eastern side of the Lizard Peninsula made it an ideal location for smuggling, but todays activities are limited to small fishing boats potting for shellfish out of the tiny harbour that dates back to 1784. The former lifeboat house is now in use as a restaurant, but with its slipway it is a classic reminder of the service that the RNLI has provided over the years. The nearby Manacle rocks and reef are the main reason a lifeboat was stationed here originally, but a new base at Kilcobben Cove now covers the area.

CADGWITH COVE has little protection from the southeasterly seas, with the local fishing boats engaged in the shellfish trade being winched up the beach out of harm's way. It is the classic Cornish cove and village, but its very attractiveness has made it a popular location for holiday homes. The village has held on to its history and traditions, and is in a magnificent setting, with a very well supported regatta held every year.

LIZARD POINT is the most southerly part of the British Isles, and the scene of dramatic changes in the weather, with a sea that can be calm one day, and then a boiling maelstrom of white water when the gales are blowing.

The old lifeboat house at the bottom of the cliff has a most dramatic setting, with a very steep road leading to it. Nearby the lighthouse is still operational, and the old Lloyds signal station has been restored. In the past, sailing ships coming up the channel would be given destination orders by visual signals, whilst keeping well clear of the numerous offshore rocks and reefs, not all did!!

KYNANCE has stayed a beautiful unspoilt cove under the care of the National Trust. At low tide there are superb contrasts of colour, with golden sand, green islands and cliffs, all surrounded by a translucent sea.

The little harbour at MULLION has not changed much over the years, and just offshore the island is alive with a wide variety of seabirds. The cliff walk from Mullion to Lizard Point passes along a beautiful unspoilt stretch of coastline, where little groups of ponies are sometimes grazing the cliff tops.

PORTHLEVEN is still an active fishing harbour, which until recently had its own boat building yard. With little protection from southerly winter gales, timber baulks are used to seal the harbour entrance, and a recent coastal scheme has prevented further cliff erosion. A steeply sloped beach stretches away to the south with the large lagoon of Loe Pool nearly reaching Helston.

The RINSEY area comprises an impressive stretch of coastline reaching down towards Cudden Point, and includes a collection of mine workings near Rinsey cove.
The old mine engine house of Wheal Prosper has been preserved in its disused state under the protection of the National Trust, and teams of climbers are to be frequently seen training on the cliffs.

ST MICHAELS MOUNT is a 300 foot granite outcrop just off shore from the ancient town of Marazion. A one-time monastery and place for pilgrimage, the Mount has an imposing setting in the bay and is an island at high tide. The National Trust has been responsible for its care since 1954, with thousands of visitors enjoying the gardens and castle. At low water it is possible to walk across the cobbled causeway, but a regular fleet of ferries operate back and forth from the old harbour when the tide comes in. A jewel of the Cornish coast it makes for an impressive visit whatever the weather.

PENZANCE is the major town in West Cornwall, and has also developed as the centre of transport for journeys to the Isles of Scilly, with an excellent harbour, its own heliport, and a rail link to other parts of the UK. With a superb art deco style seawater lido, and fine promenade the town is still full of character, with architecture from its bygone days, complete with granite buildings and cobbles. The harbour area boasts its own dry dock, and retains much of its historical interest.

NEWLYN is the busiest fishing port in Cornwall, and boats of all sizes operate from here. The original medieval harbour is still in use, but over the years three new piers have been constructed to cater for the large number of craft. A fish festival is now held during the summer, and the RNLI have stationed one of the new breed of fast stay- afloat vessels here to cover the area. Newlyn has certainly adapted to keep up with changing requirements, and when the fleet unloads in the early morning the fish market is a hive of activity.

MOUSEHOLE is one of the oldest Cornish harbours, and was very busy in the days of the pilchard trade. However it was also the scene of a major raid by the Spanish in 1595, when the then village was virtually destroyed by fire. Eventually the main harbour walls were built, and in the winter the entrance is sealed off from heavy seas. Nowadays the only invasion is by tourists during the summer, and also in December for the Christmas lights display.

LAMORNA COVE is set at the mouth of a beautiful green wooded valley, and for many years was one of the most important granite quarries in West Cornwall. Lamorna granite has built lighthouses around Cornwall and was also used in the old Waterloo Bridge in London. The rugged coastline and the scenic valley make the spot a popular venue for visitors, and divers enjoy exploring the cove's clear waters.

PORTHCURNO and the Minack Theatre sit in a magnificent location at the end of a green valley. Overlooking the beach, the Minack was opened in 1935, and is famous for its summer plays. Porthcurno was an important link with overseas before the advent of radio and satellite, with many of our telephone cables from abroad coming ashore at its beautiful cove. Nowadays fibre optics have replaced the heavy-duty armoured cables, but the clean sand and clear water make it a popular beach.

LANDS END is the most westerly point on mainland British Isles, and its reputation brings visitors from all over the world to see the Atlantic-sculptured cliffs and spectacular sunsets. The famous First and Last House is a popular place for tourists, and on clear days the Isles of Scilly can be seen. In recent times the complex has been extended, and a small animal farm is a popular attraction. However, the real Lands End is where the Atlantic swell pounds into the shear cliffs, whilst just off shore the impressive Long Ships Lighthouse is still in use to warn passing ships.

SENNEN COVE is directly exposed to the mighty Atlantic Ocean, with the surf breaking on the beach of Whitesand Bay making an impressive sight, and a popular surfing spot. Small fishing boats still operate out of the tiny harbour, and the RNLI station a fast offshore lifeboat here. This peaceful setting has also been used to bring ashore the new generation of fibre optic cables from across the ocean.

CAPE CORNWALL is located between Sennen Cove and Botallack Head, and remains an unspoiled headland jutting out into the Atlantic. The chimneystack is all that remains of the old Cape Cornwall mine, and today serves as a useful navigation mark to shipping in the area. Small fishing boats are still operating from Priest's Cove, and the craft are winched up the slipway to avoid the rough seas that can pound this part of the coastline. The original fishermen's huts built into the cliffs are a reminder of the cove's history.

BOTALLACK HEAD to PENDEEN is predominantly a mining area, with some of the workings stretching out under the sea. The Crowns engine houses at the bottom of the cliffs symbolise the ruggedness of Cornwall's mining history. Nearby the old Geevor mine is now a museum, and at the Levant engine house perched on the cliff edge, the original working steam engine is also well worth a visit. Located between Cape Cornwall and Pendeen Light, this section of coast is both spectacular and a dramatic reminder of Cornwall's working heritage.

ST IVES is a world famous resort renowned for its beaches, harbour, and artist colony. In earlier times a considerable industry was based on pilchard fishing and coastal trade, and whilst many fishing craft still operate from here, the harbour is now also very popular with pleasure boats. The famous lifeboats based here are launched by tractor with trailer units, and are available at all states of the tide. It was the quality and clarity of the light that attracted the original artists, and now Tate St Ives has its position overlooking Porthmeor beach.

HAYLE was one of the few available harbours on the north coast, and developed into a major industrial centre of its time, with foundries, engineering works, and a huge dynamite works providing employment for thousands. Steam engines built by the famous Harveys of Hayle served all over the world, with a flourishing shipbuilding industry complimenting the other services. Having negotiated the ever-changing sand banks, the trading ships would bring in coal and wood, plus other supplies, then take on copper and tin ore to be smelted in Wales. Nowadays the dunes and towans to the east are a magnet for visitors enjoying a chalet or camping holiday, whilst across the estuary the beaches of Carbis Bay add to this magnificent sweep of sand that is a feature of the area.

GWITHIAN and GODREVY are situated at the eastern end of the Hayle beaches, with the automated lighthouse on Godrevy Island still in use as a beacon warning of the offshore reefs. The area around the headland and cliffs are under the care of the National Trust. This unspoilt location is popular with both walkers and water users, with its many sandy inlets and rock pools. A thriving seal colony use the local coves and caves. The former sand works behind the beach at Gwithian has been regenerated as a nature reserve with several pools, and nearby the old round coastguard lookout now surrounded by chalets has become a welcome stop known as the Jam Pot Café.

PORTREATH harbour owes its existence to the mining trade, although small fishing craft still operate out of here. Sailing ships from Wales would bring coal in to unload, and take back copper and tin ore for the smelting works. A cable incline and tramway were utilised to connect to the local mining area. Because of the difficulty in entering the harbour, many ships were lost over the years, as the rugged coastline either side offers little protection.

PERRANPORTH with its fine stretch of beach and dunes has made it an ideal venue for the tourists, and with the Atlantic rollers, surfing has become a popular pastime. Hidden amongst the sand dunes is the lost church of St Piran, reputed to be the earliest Christian building in England. The town has its own airfield perched on the nearby cliffs where visitors can enjoy a scenic flight around the area.

ST AGNES' history is deeply rooted in the numerous mines in the area, and attempts were made to use the local cove of Trevaunance as a harbour. Indeed the remains of the granite pier can be seen through the clear water, having been demolished by numerous northerly gales. Surrounded by rugged cliffs, the cove still has a few small fishing boats and its own inshore rescue craft.

HOLYWELL BAY is a fine stretch of golden sand surrounded by gentle green downs and grass topped cliffs. This popular holiday beach has its very own shipwreck that lies unseen for months, but can appear overnight when the wind and tides scour away several feet of sand. This location was also used for some of the opening scenes in the Bond movie; 'Die Another Day'.

THE RIVER GANNEL and CRANTOCK lie to the west of Newquay, and comprise a popular tourist beach, plus the one time shipbuilding and trading inlet of the Gannel River. The Newquay fishing fleet and trading schooners were much in evidence here before the river started to silt up due to local mining operations. Schooners could be worked upstream to Trevemper Bridge for unloading, and the remains of old wooden craft are still to be seen.

44

NEWQUAY had its origins as a fishing port, but later a tramway was constructed right on to the quay in the harbour centre, for use in connection with the china clay trade. With the coming of the main line railway, Newquay became the flagship of the Cornish Riviera, and started to expand to accommodate thousands of visitors. The Atlantic rollers have made FISTRAL Beach the surfing centre of Cornwall, with many international events held there, but the little harbour and the Gannel estuary have not changed over the years.

BEDRUTHAN STEPS is an unspoilt stretch of coast with a distinctive row of outcrops that give it its name and unusual feature. Under the stewardship of the National trust, this will stay preserved for future generations to enjoy.

WATERGATE BAY has developed as a premier location for all types of watersports and associated leisure facilities. Many events are held here, and its proximity to the expanding Cornwall airport has made it an ideal choice for quick visits to the north Cornwall coast.

TREVOSE HEAD is bordered on both sides by unspoilt coves and fine beaches, with the Victorian lighthouse still operating automatically to warn shipping of the headland and offshore rocks. The scenery around the area is magnificent for coastal walkers, and a classic example of the North Cornish coast at its best. On the eastern side of Trevose Head, the RNLI have stationed one of the latest fast offshore boats to cover this section of coastline.

ROCK sits across the water from Padstow, and has its own regular passenger ferry service that is used by its many visitors. What was a small village and stretch of beach is now a well-known venue for those seeking a select yet simple vacation. A small heliport operates during the summer months. Many sailing boats and power craft are moored here in the season, whilst to the north are the popular Daymer Bay, and the old church of St Enodoc with its bent bell tower.

PADSTOW is set on the western side of the beautiful Camel Estuary, and is a haven for shipping along this coastline. The busy harbour has its own fishing fleet, with fast speedboat rides also being available. The estuary is popular for pleasure craft, and a regular ferry service operates over to Rock. The old railway line from Wadebridge is now well known as a cycle way (Camel Trail) with hundreds of bikes making good use of the old track bed.

POLZEATH has a fine beach that looks out over Padstow Bay, and is surrounded by grass-topped cliffs with rocky coves. The Atlantic rollers make it a mecca for surfing, with great coastal walks available on both sides. To the north Pentire Head is under the care of the National Trust, with a vist to Daymer Bay or Rock available by walking along the coastal path that follows the Camel estuary. Easy access and parking have made this a major tourist spot, but it has not spoilt the spectacular setting.

PORT ISSAC is a fishing harbour that dates back to the middle ages, with its first breakwater being built during the reign of Henry V111. Later years saw its use for the export of slate from the huge Delabole quarry, but today it is still in use by small craft. The visitors like the unspoilt 'time warp' setting of the village; whilst it is also a popular location for TV and film productions.

TINTAGEL is King Arthur country, with the local area steeped in folklore and legends. The remains of Iron Age forts and early settlements are to be found on the island, together with the ancient castle. With old quarries set into the cliffs on the mainland, this is an interesting and rugged location, with parts of the area under the protection of the National Trust.

BOSCASTLE sits in a dramatic cleft in Cornwall's north coast, and has a natural harbour that dates back to the Middle Ages. Fishing boats still use the available shelter, and the area is little changed from its early days. It was the scene of devastation in 2004 when torrential rain caused a flash flood to rip through the village causing severe damage and carrying many cars out to sea. A major reconstruction exercise has provided improved protection for the future, and restored the village to its original peaceful setting.

BUDE is a very popular resort that was once a trading port with a canal link to the inland town of Launceston. The old lock gates are still there, and make an interesting sight with the canal winding away inland through the green fields. The coming of the railway opened up the area for tourists who have made good use of the fine beaches, but happily the town has still retained its character and is a popular location. The location also marks the change from Cornwall to Devon, with the geology of the coast showing the difference.

OVER CORNWALL

Prints from this publication are available via e-mail enquiry at
overcornwall@yahoo.co.uk
The minimum print size is 18 x12 inches
Quotes for commercial use for brochure/advertising can also be given on request